MW01489801

i.t.a. Linguistic Readers

bʊk 3

Jane Flynn Anderson, Ph.D.

Initial Teaching Alphabet Foundation
New York, NY
2017

Adapted from
Early-to-Read i/t/a/ Program-Revised

Harold J. Tanyzer, Ph.D.
and
Albert J. Mazurkiewicz, Ed.D.

Initial Teaching Alphabet Publications
New York NY
1963, 1966

contents

kim

kim ran out uv thu hous. hee
ſhut thu dœr with u baŋ! hee kikt thu
step. hee kikt thu fens. kim did not
smiel. hee did not laf. kim wuꙅ mad.

his muthr cauld, "kim, pleeꙅ
cum bak in and pik up yœr thiŋꙅ."

"whie dω ie hav tω dω evreething?" kim sed tω himself. "aul ie dω iƨ pωt uwæ, pωt uwæ, pωt uwæ."

"did yω heer mee, kim? cauld hiƨ muthr.

kim did not heer wel when hee did not waunt tω dω whut hiƨ muthr askt. hee cωd heer betr when hee waunted tω dω sumthing els.

"kim," hiƨ muthr cauld ugen.

"ie'm cuming," sed kim.

"kim, it iƨ cleening tiem," sed his muthr. "pleeƨ help bie pωting uwæ yœr thingƨ."

kim started tω pωt his things
uwæ. hee pωt his cars in u boks.
then hee tωk out his red car. hee
ran thu car on thu ʃhelf. hee ran thu
car on thu boks.

"kim," sed his muthr. "pωt
yœr cars uwæ." kim pωt thu
car intω thu boks ugen. hee pikt
up u whisl. hee blω thu whisl.

"kim!" cauld his muthr.

kim pωt thu whisl intω thu
boks. hee pikt up sum bωks. hee
pωt them on thu ʃhelf. thu top bωk
wus ubout an ærplæn. kim started
tω reed it.

"kim!" cauld his muthr ugen.
sœ kim pʊt thu bʊk on thu ʃhelf.

cɑrs and whisls and bʊks—
tækiŋ tois ɑut is fun. pʊtiŋ them
bak is wrk.

"kim," sed his muthr.

"whut can ʃhee waunt nɑu?"
kim sed tʊ himself.

"thaŋks fœr helpiŋ," sed
muthr.

kim ran ɑut uv thu hɑus. hee
felt betr. his muthr felt betr aulsœ.

sam and kathee

this is kathee and this is sam,
thu big farm hoers. wun dæ fathr
let kathee ried sam too toun. uwæ
thæ went—sam and kathee.

ŧhær w/r menɛɛ pɛɛpl in toun. u band wuꙅ plæiᶇ and ŧhu bulωn man wuꙅ ŧhær. ŧhu man had red, yelœ, and blω bulωnꙅ.

"wæt, sam," sed kaŧhɛɛ. "dœn't wauk nou. hɛɛr cumꙅ u puræd. ie liek pu[ædꙅ."

men in red, yelœ, and blω cœts cæm bie. ŧhæ had menɛɛ flagꙅ. ŧhæ w/r ŧhu band. ŧhu band wuꙅ plæiᶇ and mar[hiᶇ.

sam'ꙅ fɛɛt started tω gœ up and doun. ŧhen sam bɛɛgan tω mar[h. sam and kaŧhɛɛ w/r in ŧhu puræd!

"œ, sam," sed kaþɛɛ. "yʊ ar not u puræd hœrs. yʊ ar u farm hœrs. yʊ canot bɛɛ in u puræd. stop, sam, stop!"

sam did not stop. on hɛɛ waukt wiþ kaþɛɛ in þu puræd. up hil and dɑun--bie þu skʊl, bie þu zʊ.

"whut wil ie dʊ?" sed kaþɛɛ. "hɑu can ie mæk sam gœ hœm tʊ þu farm?"

just þen þu puræd went bie u stœr. u man cæm ɑut. "hɛɛr, sam," hɛɛ sed. "hav an apl."

sam lʊkt at þu red apl, and hɛɛ lʊkt at þu puræd. sam liekt þu puræd and aul þu pɛɛpl in it.

hee liekt aul thu flægz, aul thu red, yelœ, and blœ cœts, and aul thu bulœnz. best uv aul, sam liekt thu band.

but sam liekt aplz, tœ. and hee waunted sumthing tœ eet. sœ sam stopt tœ eet thu apl.

uwæ went thu puræd. and uwæ went sam and kathee, hœm tœ thu farm.

ţhu yœ-yœ contest

"cum on, bob," cauld rikɛɛ.

"ţhær iʒ gœirŋ tѡ bɛɛ u yœ-yœ

contest. it iʒ at ţhu plægrѻund on

yœr strɛɛt. wɛɛ can trie tѡ win u

nѡ biek."

"ie waunt tω bee in thu contest," cauld bob. "ie want tω win u nω biek. ie am gœiŋ tω lωk fœr mie yœ-yœ."

whær wus bob's yœ-yœ? hee lωkt and lωkt. hee lωkt evreewhær. hee did not fiend thu yœ-yœ. bob's yœ-yœ wus laust!

"hav yω lωkt in thu yard, bob?" sed muthr. "get yœr cœt and lωk in thu yard."

whær wus bob's cœt? bob lωkt uround. hee did not fiend his cœt.

"mie yœ-yœ iꟗ laust and nou mie cœt iꟗ laust," sed bob.

bob ran tw̃ thu yard. hɛɛ lʊkt and lʊkt. hɛɛ lʊkt evrɛɛwhæer. hiꟗ yœ-yœ wuꟗ not thæer. hiꟗ yœ-yœ wuꟗ stil laust.

bob ran doun thu strɛɛt. hɛɛ ran tw̃ thu plæground.

"ar yw̃ gœein̄ tw̃ bɛɛ in thu yœ-yœ contest?" cauld rikɛɛ.

"nœ," sed bob. "ie can't fiend mie yœ-yœ."

11

ŧhu gœlɖ riŋ

"cum on, ʃhaun, ŧhu carnivul haʐ cum tωⱳ tᴕun," seɖ jæmʐ.

"græt!" seɖ ʃhaun. "ie waunt tωⱳ rieɖ on ŧhu mærɛɛ-gœ-rᴕund."

ʃhaun and jæmʒ ran doun ŧhu street. ŧhæ ran too ŧhu midl uv ŧhu toun. ŧhær wuʒ ŧhu carnivul, and ŧhær wɾ aul ŧhu riedʒ.

jæmʒ lookt sad.

"doo yoo hav enɛɛ munɛɛ, jæmʒ?" sed ʃhaun.

"noe," sed jæmʒ sadlɛɛ. "doo yoo hav munɛɛ fœr u ried?"

"ɨe hav munɛɛ fœr wun ried," sed ʃhaun. nou ʃhaun wuʒ sad, too. hɛɛ waunted u ried, but hɛɛ waunted hiʒ frend too hav u ried aulsœ.

"hɾɛɛ! hɾɛɛ!" cauld ŧhu mærɛɛ-gœ-round man. "gœ fœr u ried.

win u fr∈ ried if yω get ɪʰu gœld riɳ."

"ie hœp yω get ɪʰu gœld riɳ, ʃhaun," sed jæmʃ.

"ie hœp sœ, tω," sed ʃhaun. "if ie get ɪʰu gœld riɳ, yω can have ɪʰu fr∈ ried."

"hɾ∈! hɾ∈!" cauld ɪʰu mær∈-gœ-round man.

ʃhaun gæv ɪʰu man hiʃ mun∈. h∈ got on u big brəun hœrs. up and dəun went ɪʰu big brəun hœrs. up and dəun went ʃhaun.

ɪʰu mær∈-gœ-round went urəund and urəund.

uround and uround went ʃhaun. hee sau thu gœld ring.

"get it, ʃhaun! get thu ring!" cauld jæmz.

ʃhaun pωt out hiz hand, and caut thu gœld ring.

"ie got it!" ʃhouted ʃhaun.hee wuz væree eksieted.

"hωræ!" ʃhouted jæmz. nou hee cωd hav u ried, tω.

cɔubɔi seecret

jaksun wus u cɔubɔi. hee had u cɔubɔi sωt. hee had u cɔubɔi hat. hee had u cɔubɔi hɔers. hee sang liek u cɔubɔi. hee wus u cɔubɔi aul thu tiem!

wun dæ muthr sed, "tiem
fœr scœl, jaksun. plɛɛs pœt on
yœr scœl clœs."

jaksun sed, "ie can't wær mie
scœl clœs. ie am u couboi! ie nɛɛd
tœ wær mie couboi sœt!"

auf hɛɛ went tœ scœl in his
couboi sœt.

thu nekst dæ muthr sed, "tiem
fœr chrch, jaksun. plɛɛs pœt on
yœr chrch sœt."

jaksun sed, "ie can't wær mie
chrch sœt. ie am u couboi! ie nɛɛd
tœ wær mie couboi sœt!" auf hɛɛ
went tœ chrch in his couboi sœt.

on friedæ muthr sed, "tiem
fœr u partee, jaksun. plees pwt on
yœr partee clœz."

jaksun sed, "ie can't wær
partee clœz. ie am u couboi! ie need
tw wær mie couboi swt!"

auf hee went tw thu partee in
his couboi swt.

wun dæ u man cæm tw see
jaksun's fathr. hee wuz u væree
taul man. his fæs wuz brnd bie thu
sun. hee wœr u broun swt.

fathr sed, "jaksun, this is teks.
hee is u couboi tw."

jaksun lʊkt at teks. hɛɛ lʊkt at his sunbɾnd fæs and brɑun sʊot.

"whær iꙅ yœr cɑubɑi sʊot?" jaksun askt teks.

"hɑem," sed teks.

"whær iꙅ yœr cɑubɑi hœrs?" askt jaksun.

"hɑem," sed teks. "ie cæm in mie cɑr."

"wel," sed jaksun. "ie dœn't Ꝯhiŋk yʊo ɑr u rɛɛl cɑubɑi."

"whut if ie tel yʊo u cɑubɑi stɑerɛɛ?" sed teks. hɛɛ tɑeld u stɑerɛɛ ubɑut u hœrs Ꝯhat ran uwæ. it wuꙅ u værɛɛ funɛɛ stɑerɛɛ.

"wel," sed jaksun. "ie stil dœn't beeleev yœ ar u reel cœuboi."

"œ.kæ." sed teks. "supœs ie plæ yœ u cœuboi saung?" teks sæng u cœuboi saung. it wus u sad saung.

"ie stil dœn't beeleev yœ ar u reel cœuboi," sed jaksun.

"wel, nœu," sed teks. "ŧhær is œnlee wun ŧhing ie can dœ. tœmorœ ie hav tœ fiks fenses. hœu ubœut gœeing wiŧh mee?"

ŧhu nekst dæ, jaksun went wiŧh teks. hee wœer his cœuboi sœt.

teks wœr u cɶubɔi sɷt. hɛɛ
wœr u cɶubɔi hat. hɛɛ rœd̦ u hœrs.
hɛɛ lɷkt liek u cɶubɔi!

jaksun had̦ u gɷd̦ dæ wiþ
teks. hɛɛ rœd̦ u cɶubɔi hœrs. þæ
d̦id̦ cɶubɔi wɹk. hɛɛ æt u cɶubɔi
lunᴄh wiþ ᵺu uthɹ cɶubɔiʐ.

at ᵺu end̦ uv ᵺu dæ teks
askt, "nɶu d̦ɷ yɷ bɛɛlɛɛv ie am u
cɶubɔi, jaksun?"

"yes," sed̦ jaksun. nɶu ie
bɛɛlɛɛv yɷ ar u rɛɛl cɶubɔi. yestɹdæ
yɷ lɷkt liek sumwun hɷ wɹks in
an ofis. nɶu yɷ lɷk liek u cɶubɔi."

teks laft. "wel, nou," hee sed.
"let mee tel you u litl seecret. ie liek
beeig u coubɔi. thær is nuthig ie
wood rathr bee. but yestrdæ wus
mie dæ auf. eeven u coubɔi needs u
dæ auf wuns in u whiel."

sins then, jaksun is stil u
coubɔi. hee stil wærs u coubɔi soot.
hee stil wærs u coubɔi hat. hee stil
rieds u coubɔi hɔers. but not aul thu
tiem!

mɔest dæs hee gɔes too scool.
then hee wærs his scool clɔes.

when hee gɔes too chrch, hee
wærs his chrch clɔes.

sumtiems hee goes tw u partee.
then hee wærs his partee cloes.

and sumtiems hee plæs
couboi. then hee wærs his couboi
cloes!

yw see, jaksun noes u seecret.
eeven u couboi needs u dæ auf
wuns in u whiel!

samee thu sɾcus seel

samee wuz u seel. hee livd with
uthɾ seels in u sɾcus. thu uthɾ seels
did triks in thu sɾcus—but not
samee. samee cωd not dω triks liek
thu uthɾ seels. sœ samee wuz sad.

wun dæ u hapєє clɔun cæm
bie. thu clɔun sau samєє lʊkiŋ
sadlєє at thu uthr sєєls. thu sєєls
wʌr dansiŋ and bɔunsiŋ bauls up
intʊ thu ær. thu hapєє clɔun did
not liek tʊ sєє samєє sad.

sœ thu clɔun bєєgan tʊ
dans. hєє pikt samєє up and danst
urɔund and urɔund with him. sʊn
samєє waunted tʊ dans bie
himself.

samєє bєєgan tʊ dans. thu
clɔun danst, tʊ. as thu clɔun danst,
u bel cæm auf his ʃhʊ. samєє
danst aftr thu bel. hєє bɔunst thu
bel on his nœs. hєє bɔunst and
danst.

uraund and uraund hee danst,
baunsiŋ thu bel. it wuz fun.

thu nekst dæ thu claun taust
samee an œrunj. samee baunst thu
œrunj on hiz nœz. then hee taust
thu œrunj intω thu ær.

œ, nœ! this tiem hee mist, sœ
hee started œvʌr ugen. hee taust thu
bel, then thu œrunj, then thu bel
ugen. dæ aftʌr dæ, samee danst
and baunst and taust.

wun dæ thu claun hid thu bel.
samee lωkt and lωkt fœr it. hee
lωkt evreewhær, and at last hee
found it. samee started dansiŋ and
baunsiŋ thu bel ugen.

az hee danst, hee sau thu œrunj. swn hee wus bounsiŋ thu bel and thu œrunj at thu sæm tiem.

then hee sau u cœcunut. hee bounst thu cœcunut on his nœs, tw. samee danst fastr and fastr. hee taust his tois hier and hier.

wun dæ samee sau bois and grls wachiŋ him. that dæ samee nw hee wus u gwd srucs seel. hee cwd dw triks. hee wus væree hapee!

aftr that dæ samee danst fastr and fastr. hee taust his tois hier and hier. nou hee wus u hapee seel.

hee did his triks sœ wel that peepl waunted him tꙣ bee on teluviȝun!

nꙩu samee is u teluviȝun star! hee is u hapee sⲅcus seel hꙣ dus menee triks. his frend, thu hapee clꙩun, helps him dꙣ triks. thæ ar bœth teluviȝun stars.

rap! rap! rap!

wuns an œld man went intω thu wωds. hεε cæm tω an œld hous in thu wωds.

thu œld hous had nœ dœrs and nœ windœs. nœwun livd in thu œld brœken hous.

thu œld man went intω thu
œld hous. up thu œld steps hεε
went, intω thu œld brœken hous.

suddenlεε hεε hₐrd sumᵗhiᵑ! it
went rap! rap! rap! whut wuₛ that
noiₛ?

thu noiₛ wuₛ upstæerₛ in thu
œld hous. thu œld man waunted
tω fiend out whut thu noiₛ wuz. sœ
hεε went up thu stæerₛ.

(bεε cæerful, œld man! dœn't
faul on thu œld, œld steps!)

hεε lωkt in thu fₐrst bedrωm.
nuᵗhiᵑ thæer!

hεε lωkt in thu secund
bedrωm. nuᵗhiᵑ thæer!

hee lʊkt in thu thɪrd bedrʊʊm. nuthiŋ thæer eethɪr!

whut wuʒ that rap, rap, rap? whæer wuʒ that noiʒ cumiŋ frum?

then thu œld man hɪrd it ugen. rap! rap! rap! it cæm frum thu atic.

up thu atic stæerʒ went thu œld man.

(bee cæerful, œld man! lʊk out fœr thu œld atic steps!)

up, up, up went thu œld man. in thu atic hee hɪrd thu noiʒ ugen. rap! rap! rap!

it wuʒ getiŋ loudɪr! **rap! rap! rap!** whut wuʒ that noiʒ?

(bee cærful, œld man! yoo
dœn't nœ whut it iz!)

 thu noiz wuz on u ſhelf, væree
loud! sœ hee waukt œvﬧ too thu
ſhelf.

rap! rap! rap!

it wuz rapiŋ pæpﬧ!

whut u jœk on thu œld man!
whut u jœk on yoo!

jak and thu bæbee brds

jak did not noe whut too doo.
thær wus noebudee on thu strεεt.
thær wus noebudee at thu
plægraund. noebudee wus plæiŋ
in enεε uv thu yards.

jak wus aul oloen. hεε thaut
and thaut. whut cood hεε doo?

jak wuz bœrd, sœ he sat undɹ u treε. heε lʊkt up and sau u robin'z nest in ᵺu treε.

"ie wundɹ if ᵺu robin haz eneε bæbeε bɹrdz," heε ᵺaut. "ie wundɹ if ie can seε sum bæbeε robinz in ᵺu nest."

jak wuz cʊreεus, sœ heε started tʊ cliem ᵺu treε. it wuz εεzeε tʊ cliem up ᵺat treε. heε had cliemd up ᵺu treε meneε tiemz beεfœr.

jak cliemd ɷut on u branch. heε waunted tʊ lʊk intʊ ᵺu bɹrd'z nest. heε waunted tʊ seε if ᵺær wɹr bæbeε bɹrdz in ᵺu nest.

just then thu muthr robin flω
bak tω thu nest and sau jak. ʃhɛɛ
did not nœ that jak just waunted
tω lωk at hr bæbɛɛs. ʃhɛɛ thaut jak
waunted tω hrt them. with u
scrɛɛʧh, thu muthr robin flω at jak.

when thu robin flω at him, jak
wuʃ srpriezd. hɛɛ wuʃ sœ srpriezd
that hɛɛ fel out uv thu trɛɛ. doun,
doun, doun hɛɛ fel. hɛɛ landed on
his arm.

"ou! ou!" cried jak. "mie arm!
ie hrt mie arm."

jak's muthr cæm runiŋ.

"whut is thu matr, jak? whut
wr yω dωiŋ?" ʃhɛɛ sed.

"ie cliemd up thu tree tω see thu bæbee brds, but ie fel dσun," sed jak, "σu! ie hrt mie arm."

jak's muthr lωkt at his arm. "ie dœn't think yœr arm is brœken, jak, but let's hav u doctr tæk u lωk at it," ʃhee sed.

muthr tωk jak tω see thu doctr.   .

"whut is thu matr, jak?" thu doctr askt.

jak beegan. "nœbudee wus urσund. evreebudee but mee had sumthing tω dω. sœ ie cliemd up u tree..."

jak stopt. hee lukt wreed. "is
mie arm broeken, doctr?" jak wus
ufræd.

"noe, jak," sed thu doctr.
"yoer arm is not broeken, but it wil
hrt foer u fue dæs. yoo can goe
hoem nou, but doen't cliem up that
tree ugen!"

ꝼhu stœrm

ꝺwæn wuꙅ in beꝺ, but hꬲ wuꙅ
not slꬲpiꞃ. it wuꙅ u hot niet, sœ it
wuꙅ harꝺ tꙍ gœ tꙍ slꬲp. hꬲ wuꙅ
not slꬲpꬲ, sœ ꝺwæn ꝼhaut ubout
whut hꬲ waunteꝺ tꙍ bꬲ when hꬲ
grꙍ up.

"ie am gœiŋ tꙍ bεε u fierman when ie grœ up," hεε cauld tꙍ his muthɼ and faᴛhɼ. "can u fierman stæ up aul niet?"

"u fierman can't stæ up aul niet. u fierman nεεds slεεp," cauld faᴛhɼ.

"count ᴛhu stars and yꙍ wil gœ tꙍ slεεp," cauld muthɼ.

"it wil tæk mεε aul niet tꙍ count ᴛhu stars," sed dwæn as hεε bεεgan. "wun, tꙍ, ᴛhrεε..."

wun star lꙍkt red. it wus mꙍviŋ. as dwæn waᴄht, ᴛhu star flꙍ uwæ.

"œ," þaut dwæn. "þhat's not u stɑr. it's an ærplæn. it's u big jet."

sωn dwæn fel uslɛp. hɛ drempt hɛ wuꝫ flieiŋ u big jet. hɛ wuꝫ tækiŋ pɛpl whær þhæ waunted tω gœ. it wuꝫ fun.

but dwæn cωd not sɛ whær hɛ wuꝫ flieŋ þhu plæn. "whær ɑr þhu stɑrꝫ?" hɛ þhaut.

þhær wɹ big clɑudꝫ in þhu skie. þhu plæn wuꝫ flieiŋ intω þhu clɑudꝫ. sωn it bɛgan tω ræn—hɑrd!

þhu wind blω and þhu ræn fel. þhu wind blω and blω.

"wee ran intoo u stœrm," sed dwæn too thu peepl on thu plæn. "up wee gœ, up ubuv thu clouds. up ubuv thu wind and ræn. up ubuv thu stœrm."

dwæn floo thu jet hierr up in thu skie. up, up, up it cliemd.

"nou wee ar out uv thu stœrm," sed dwæn. hee wuz flieirg thu peepl hœm.

"soon wee wil land," sed dwæn. "wee wil start flieirg doun. doun, doun, doun. that wil bee fun!"

just then dwæn wœk up. hee jumpt out uv bed.

thær wuz sumthing hee waunted tωo tel his muthr and fathr.

"when ie groe up ie'm goeing tωo flie an ærplæn," hee sed.

"whie, dwæn, yestrdæ yωo sed yωo wr goeing tωo bee u fierman," sed his muthr.

dwæn laft. "nou ie'm going tωo flie an ærplæn. ie'm goeing tωo flie u big jet."

ʄhu nɷ trumpet

pɑcœ'ᴢ fɑʄhr baut him u trumpet fœr hiᴢ brʄhdæ.

"œ bɔi," pɑcœ sed. "u trumpet iᴢ just whut ie waunted!" hee blɷ and blɷ. but nœ sound cæm out.

pacœ'z fathr ʃhœd him hou tœ plæ it. pacœ kept trieiŋ, and sœn hꜟ cꙍd plæ hiz trumpet. hꜟ lrnd tœ plæ *pop gœs thu weezl*. hꜟ plæd it œvr and œvr.

mises sanches livd in thu upartment ubuv pacœ'z familꜟ. ʃhꜟ sed tœ his muthr, "pacœ iz u nies bœi. ie liek him and ie liek muezic. ie liek *pop gœs thu weezl*, but ie am an œld lædꜟ. when hꜟ plæz it œvr and œvr, it mæks mꜟ nrvus."

pacœ'z muthr sed tœ him, "ie liek *pop gœs thu weezl*.

but you plæ ŧhu sæm tωn œvɾ
and œvɾ. it mæks mɛɛ nɾvus. it
mæks miseʒ sanɕheʒ nɾvus. it iʒ
tω loud."

pacœ'ʒ sistɾ murɛɛu sed, "ie
ugrɛɛ. yœr trumpet iʒ noizɛɛ."

pacœ tœld hiʒ faŧhɾ, "mie
muezic mæks miseʒ sanɕheʒ
nɾvus. mirɛɛu seʒ it's tω noizɛɛ.
ɛɛven muŧhɾ ŧhiŋks it's tω loud."

pacœ's faŧhɾ sed, "trie plæiŋ
in ŧhu clozet. ŧhen it wœn't sound
sœ loud."

pacœ ŧhaut, "mie muezic
wœn't mæk ŧhu cœts nɾvus.

ᴛhu bœts wœn't ᴛhiŋk it's
tꙍ loud. ᴛhu clozet is u gꙍd
plæs tꙍ plæ mie nꙍ trumpet."

pacœ went intꙍ ᴛhu clozet
and clœzd ᴛhu dœr. hᴇᴇ plæd hiꙅ
trumpet.

"ᴛhat's betᵣ," evrᴇᴇwun sed.
"it's not sœ loud nou."

sœ pacœ plæd *pop gœꙅ ᴛhu
wᴇᴇzl* œvᵣ and œvᵣ ugen in ᴛhu
clozet. nou evrᴇᴇwun iꙅ hapᴇᴇ.

Appendix A

Notes to Teachers and Parents

Why a linguistic version of i.t.a. readers?

In 1959, Sir James Pitman introduced a simplified, phonetic alphabet for teaching beginning reading. His motivation for doing so was the complexity of written English: although there are only 26 letters in the traditional alphabet, there are 44 sounds and more than 1,100 different spelling combinations.

Because Pitman believed that children needed a transition bridge from reading phonetically-regular text to the complex orthography of written English, he built in some spelling conventions, e.g., retaining double letters and "y" endings for words like "pretty, happy." This resulted in i.t.a. readers that did not represent a true linguistic approach.

This version is a linguistic adaptation of the original Early-to-Read books published by the Initial Teaching Alphabet Foundation. It incorporates what we know about the link between speech sounds and the written representations of those sounds in the beginning stages of literacy development.

We now know that young children who are on a normal developmental path to literacy acquisition will spell unknown words by sound (e.g., *sed* for *said*), mapping the speech sounds they hear to the letters that represent those sounds. At the same time, they are seeing *said* in their readers. Soon, these two images are hooked together in their lexicon, so that anytime they see *said* they automatically and unconsciously pronounce *sed*.

Children at risk of reading failure do not acquire these phonological speech-to-print connections. This linguistic book series is designed to help them "crack the code" of English. By reading the phonetically-regular text of the initial teaching alphabet, they internalize the sound spellings of English, facilitating the connection between what a word looks like in traditional orthography (TO) and what it sounds like (i.t.a.).

What's new in these linguistic readers?

While the original stories of the Early-to-Read i/t/a/ Program have been retained, some have been moved to different book levels based on syntactical complexity. Syntax has also been modified to reflect more authentic speech patterns, while keeping the words-per-sentence ratio low in the first three books.

The original stories have also been updated to reflect the new generation of children and families from many different cultures and ethnicities that make up the population of the United States.

In addition, more accurate contemporary information has required revision of some stories, for example, the story of the First Thanksgiving. Finally, illustrations have been reduced to one per story in order to encourage mental construction of story narratives rather than guessing words from pictures based on illustrations on every page as in the original i.t.a. readers.

Who are these linguistic readers for?

These readers were developed to assist the literacy development of three groups: (1) young children at risk of reading failure; (2) older students and adults with dyslexia/reading disabilities, and (3) speakers of other languages learning to read and write English.

Children at-risk of reading failure. If children are on track for normal reading acquisition, by kindergarten age they will be able to map speech sounds to print by writing words the way they sound, e.g., *luv, wuz, sed.*

Children who cannot analyze spoken words by segmenting, blending, and deleting syllables and sounds do not make these speech to print matches and are at risk of reading failure. Drilling them on isolated letters, sounds, or word families does not fix their underlying phonological deficit. What they need are significant exposure to phonetically-regular words in authentic sentence patterns, embedded in coherent stories. These new linguistic readers, accompanied by a creative writing protocol that emphasizes spelling by sound using i.t.a., will give them what they need.

Children and adults with dyslexia: Because English orthography is complex, the incidence of dyslexia in English is estimated to be twice that of transparent languages like Italian or German, where sounds map to letters more consistently.

Figure 1 shows how phonological deficits affect every aspect of reading development. It is only through correction of the underlying deficit in the phonological component of language that dyslexic students will become truly proficient readers. And the longer they progress through school without appropriate intervention, the greater the deficit in all the higher reading processes, particularly comprehension, vocabulary, and background knowledge.

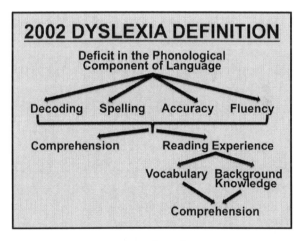

Figure 1: International Dyslexia Association 2002 definition of dyslexia

Based on 30 years of research and clinical practice, we know that reading and writing phonetically with the initial teaching alphabet is the key to correcting the underlying phonological deficit at the core of reading failure (Flynn & Deering, 1993; Flynn, 2000; Flynn & Rahbar, 2017). The original i.t.a. readers, the Early-to Read series of the 1960s, have been used successfully for remediation of those children who have failed to conquer the challenge of English.

But many teachers and students themselves have noted inconsistencies in the Early-to-Read books because they did not follow the single sound-single letter principle that would best remediate their phonological deficit.

This linguistic series is designed to fix that problem. Using i.t.a., students will continue to write the sounds that they hear, and they will now see that same phonetic transcription of words in their i.t.a. readers.

English language learners. English is considered one of the most difficult languages to learn because sounds do not map consistently to specific letters; for example, the long /a/ can be spelled *a, ai, a_e, ay, ea, eigh,* or *aigh.* i.t.a. solves this problem in the beginning stage of learning English by replicating the process that young English-speaking children follow: spelling words the way they sound. In i.t.a., the long /a/ sound is always represented by one symbol, æ, so there is no confusion about how to pronounce words with long /a/, no matter how the word is spelled in traditional orthography.

This is accomplished is with an i.t.a. sound-symbol chart (Figure 2) that English learners always have in front of them as they write.

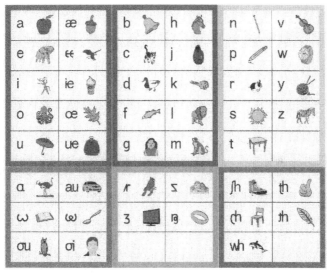

Figure 2: i.t.a. sound chart

This i.t.a. sound-symbol chart is also helpful for learning the pronunciation of English sounds that do not exist in an English learner's native language. For example, /th/ does not exist in Spanish, and is usually pronounced /d/. Practicing the sound connected to the picture helps English learners master English phonology.

The essence of why i.t.a. helps English learners was expressed by a Ph.D. biostatistician, a native of Iran who was perfectly fluent in English. On being presented with the i.t.a. chart and how it was used with dyslexics, he asked, "Why didn't I learn English this way?

How to use these linguistic readers

For the past 30 years, the Initial Teaching Alphabet Foundation has supported research using the original i.t.a. readers with dyslexic children and adults. The results support the use of i.t.a. reading and writing for remediation of reading disability/dyslexia (Lyon & Flynn, 1991; Flynn & Deering, 1993; Flynn, 2000; Flynn & Rahbar, 2017; Meyer & Felton, 1999).

In research settings, literacy clinics, and schools, these readers are used in conjunction with an i.t.a. writing protocol where students write all words exactly as they sound by using the i.t.a. symbols.

For information on the i.t.a. writing protocol, visit http://itafoundation.org/reading/writing/writing/

These linguistic readers are designed to be used with the reading protocol we used in our reseach, Repeated Oral Assisted Reading (Flynn, 2000). Repeated Oral Assisted Reading (ROAR) is based on the National Reading Panel meta-analysis of studies focused on improving fluency for developing and struggling readers.

Mandated by Congress to analyze the research on what works for reading development, the panel concluded that guided oral re-reading was the key to developing the automaticity needed to free cognitive resources for comprehension of what is read (National Reading Panel, 2000).

Figure 3 summarizes our first research study contrasting i.t.a. reading-writing with two prominent phonics approaches: Orton-Gillingham (Project Read) and DISTAR (Reading Mastery). After nine months of intervention, children in the i.t.a. program achieved significantly-higher accuracy and fluency gains, even though they were tested with passages written in traditional orthography (Flynn, 2000; Flynn &Deering, 1993).

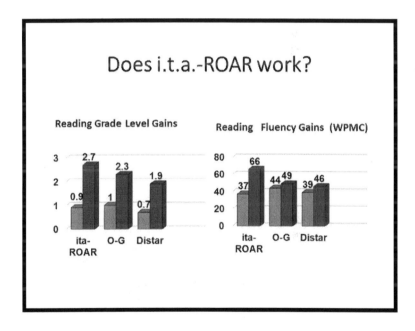

Figure 3: Reading Gains after Nine Months of Intervention

Appendix B

Repeated Oral Assisted Reading (ROAR) Protocol

Jane Flynn Anderson, Ph.D.

Repeated Oral Assisted Reading

Repeated Oral Assisted Reading (ROAR) is a one-on-one intervention that results, on average, in two grade levels gain in reading accuracy and comprehension if it can be implemented 3-4 times per week, in 15-minute segments, as reported in Figure 3.

The essence of ROAR is guided, repeated oral reading of instuctional-level text. We use the phonetically-regular i.t.a. texts to help students internalize the underlying sounds of English words while building their accuracy and fluency. The teacher or tutor helps the student master each sentence before moving on to the next sentence, and to longer sequences of sentences by the Gradual Release of Responsibility Process: (1) I read; (2) we read; (3) you read.

Step-by-step directions for the ROAR process is included in this section. For videos that demonstrate each step, as well as fluency charts and checklists, visit http://itafoundation.org/reading/reading-2/roar/

ROAR Protocol Checklist

Jane Flynn Anderson, Ph.D.

ROAR Pretest (One minute)

- ☐ If beginning a new story, preview it with a picture walk or brief summary
- ☐ If there are pictures, cover them up
- ☐ Point to where your student is to begin reading
- ☐ Record for one minute
- ☐ Keep track of **ALL** Deviations From Print (DFPs), including repetitions of a single word or group of words
- ☐ Do **NOT** call attention to Deviations from Print that your student has made. ROAR will correct these

Charting the Pretest (Figure 4)

- ☐ Compute Words Per Minute Correct (WPMC): total words read – Deviations From Print
- ☐ Compute Percent of Words Read Accurately (%ACC): WPMC / total words read
- ☐ Chart % ACC and WPMC in blue (Cold Read)

ROAR Practice (10-12 min.)

Ensure that your student tracks with you at every step of this practice session.
- ☐ "My turn." (I read).

- o Slide your finger smoothly under each word as you read the first sentence.
- o **Read at a normal or close-to-normal pace.** (If your student is very slow, you may start by reading slower, but you should speed up when reviewing sets of sentences.)
- ☐ "Together." (We read.)
  - o If your student stumbles on a word, keep going until the end of the sentence.
  - o Do not call attention to errors/DFPs.
  - o **Go back and repeat steps "My turn" and "Together" until your student reads fluently with you.**
- ☐ "Your turn." (You read).
  - o When your student is reading smoothly in the "We read" sequence, have him/her read the sentence alone.
  - o Repeat "My turn, Together, Your turn" if your student stumbles or reads very slowly.
- ☐ Repeat this same process with the next sentence.
- ☐ **Combine sentences to build fluency with longer segments.**

ROAR Post-Test (One Minute)

- ☐ Go back somewhere near or at the beginning of the practice session text.
- ☐ Time your student as (s)he reads for one minute.
- ☐ Keep track of Deviations From Print (DFP)

Charting the Post-Test (Figure 4)

☐ Chart WPMC and %ACC in pink (hot read)

☐ Review the chart with your student to highlight accuracy and fluency improvement.

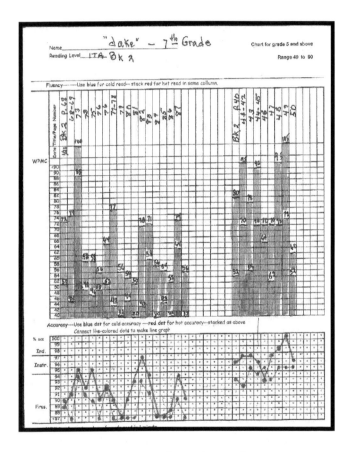

Figure 4: Student chart of pre-test and post-test fluency and accuracy

References

DIckman, E. (2017). Do we need a new definition of dyslexia? (Figure 1). International Dyslexia Association, 2002. Retrieved May 1, 2017 at https://dyslexiaida.org/do-we-need-a-new-definition-of-dyslexia.

Flynn, J., & Rahbar, M. (2017). Phonological and Orthographic Reading Disabilities: Response to Treatments Using the Initial Teaching Alphabet (i.t.a.) and Repeated Assisted Reading. Submitted for publication.

Flynn, J. (2000). The Use of the Initial Teaching Alphabet for Remediation of Dyslexia. New York: Initial Teaching Alphabet Foundation.

Flynn, J., & Deering, W. (1993). Eavesdropping on the brain: The Gundersen Medical Foundation dyslexia studies. The Gundersen Medical Journal, 1 (2), 49-54.

Lyon, G.R., and Flynn, J. (1991). Educational validation studies with subtypes of learning disabled readers. In B.P. Rourke (Ed.). Neuropsychological Validation of Learning Disability Subtypes. New York: Guilford Press, 223-242.

Meyer, M., & Felton, R. (1999). Repeated reading to enhance fluency: Old approaches and new directions. Annals of Dylexia, 49, 283-306.

National Reading Panel. (2000). **Teaching children to read:** An evidence-based assessment of the scientific research literature on reading and its implications for reading instruction. National Institute of Child Health and Human Development. Washington, D.C.

Initial Teaching Alphabet Foundation Media Resources

www.itafoundation.org. The official website of the i.t.a. Foundation includes a plethora of print and video resources for teachers and parents wishing to implement intervention programs for struggling readers.

www.itaprogramwinonasmu.org. Dr. Flynn Anderson's i.t.a. Literacy Clinic at Saint Mary's University in Winona, MN has served struggling readers since 1988. This website contains demonstration videos and reprints of Dr. Flynn Anderson's research on the use of i.t.a. with dyslexic students.

www.youtube.com/user/readingdocflynn. Dr. Flynn Anderson's YouTube channel contains demonstration videos on i.t.a. and a range of other topics regarding reading development, with a focus on English learners and those with reading disabilities/dyxslexia.